Talking u
Conversations for Life

Edited by Lynn Hutton

Contents

 Abingdon Press

Talking with Your Teen
Conversations for Life

Have you ever wished for an hour alone with a room full of parenting experts?

Then *Talking with Your Teen* was written just for you. A group of pastors and family therapists gathered together to send parents the best advice they had on communication within the family. With specialties in therapy for children and adolescents, couples therapy, family ministry, and grief counseling, the group offers practical, proven advice.

The goal of this study is to provide you:

▲ skills and understanding to help you be more confident parents
▲ help building stronger family relationships
▲ a sense of community and support from other parents in your church or community

What's in a lesson?

Each begins with an Opening Prayer and Scripture to provide the faith foundations for the study. Activities follow to build parenting skills as well as general knowledge. Skill activities offer new methods to parenting; knowledge activities provide information about topics such as child development and stages of growth.

What materials will you need?

The only tangible materials you'll need are provided in this book or will be brought by the group leader. One of your most important resources, however, will be other parents in your sessions. As you listen to each others' experiences, you'll gain more advice and support. You may want to find a partner in the class to call during the week to report successes and talk about challenges you see.

Communication

Chapter One

About this session

We are creating meaning and memory with every communication. As
we look at this topic, we need to be aware that communication includes
both the verbal and the nonverbal. If we suffer from communication
issues in a family, then nothing works as it should. We want to become
conscious of what we communicate and how we communicate it in
families. This session will help us identify communication pitfalls and
give us tools to use for effective communication with teens.

Goals to help you:

Realize the importance of good communication;
Learn the Four Commandments for better communication with children;
Identify common mistakes, common obstacles to communication with
teens.

Opening Prayer

**Teach us, O God, to choose words and
actions that build up, empower, and
encourage the children you have given us
to love. Amen.**

The Four Commandments of Communication

Commandment 1.
LISTEN MORE

What you hear is always more important than what you say.
Become a careful listener.
Talk Less.

Commandment 2.
TELL THE TRUTH

Building trust with teens is based on telling the truth.

Commandment 3.
ALLOW ALL FEELINGS TO BE EXPRESSED

Let your teens tell you how they feel.
Help teens direct frustration, anger, or disappointment to the real
issue or circumstance.

Commandment 4.
RECOGNIZE YOUR OWN DEFENSIVENESS

What in your child really sets you off? When you feel your hackles
rise suddenly, do you resort to defensive tactics like sarcasm or
stonewalling? Are some of these "hot buttons" related to your own
experience with your parents? Learn what makes you uncomfortable
so that you can respond better to your child rather than react to
your own experiences.

Conversation Starters: How To Talk to Your Teen

Make "I" statements (I respect..., I love..., I enjoy..., or even, It makes
me uncomfortable....) rather than "you" statements. "I" statements
describe your own feelings or concerns rather than making judgments
about the teen. They reflect your own position and perspective on a situation.
Ask about a friend. "How is Rebecca? What did she think about...?"
Talking about a friend is less threatening than talking about the teen's
own feelings. It can open the door to moving into a conversation about
the teen's feelings.

Ask for an opinion. "What do you think about...?" (a news item) Listen to the answer! Don't rush from hearing your teen's opinion to voicing your own.

Conversation Stoppers: How *Not to* Talk to Your Teen

"You" statements
Teen: I need a new pair of shoes.
Parent: You don't take care of the ones you have!
What's wrong: Such statements generally are accusatory and discounting. Parent does not ask for more information.
Better: What kind of shoes? Why do you need them?

Blaming
Teen: I don't ever talk to you because you are always in a bad mood.
Parent: No wonder I'm in a bad mood! All I do is clean up after you, buy you expensive sneakers, take you to lessons, blah, blah, blah.
What's wrong: Parent is not addressing the teen's concerns.
Better: That's interesting. What do you see me doing that lets you know I am in a bad mood?

Shaming
Teen: You embarrassed me in front of my friends.
Parent: I can't believe you said the things you said. I never would have talked to my parents that way.
What's wrong: Parent attacks the teen's character instead of hearing the concern.
Better: I wish that confrontation had not happened in front of your friends, too.

Explaining
Teen: I don't understand why you and dad can't agree on my curfew.
Parent: You know your dad and I couldn't agree on lots of things. That is one of the reasons we are divorced.
What's wrong: Instead of acknowledging the teen's feelings, the parent

implies "If I just explain enough, you won't feel that way anymore.

Better: I know it must be frustrating for you to have different rules at different houses.

Defending

Teen: Nobody else's parents make them come straight home after the game.

Parent: You don't know how good you've got it. I never even got to go to a game when I was your age.

What's wrong: Parent tries to avoid taking the responsibility for setting a boundary.

Better: Is that right?

Stonewalling

Teen: Why can't I go to the beach with my friends?

Parent: I'm not going to talk about this now.

What's wrong: Parent shuts down all communication. The message is clear: 1 don't want to hear from you.

Better: I am concerned for your safety. What kind of supervision will there be for you?

Exaggeration

Teen: Can I borrow $5.00 until I get next week's allowance?

Parent: You always take my money, and you never pay me back.

What's wrong: *Always* and *never* are "nag words." Never is a long time.

Better: Is this for something that can't wait until next week?

Interrupting

Teen: Dad, can I go...

Parent: You can't do anything until you clean up that room!

What's wrong: All interruptions are surefire messages to the teen that what he has to say is not important.
Better: Can you get your room cleaned before you go?

All of these conversation stoppers have two things in common: they negate the importance of the feelings of the teenager, and they divert the conversation from the real issue.

Genesis 1:1-5
In the beginning when God created the heavens and the earth, the earth was a formless void and darkness covered the face of the deep, while a wind from God swept over the face of the waters. Then God said, "Let there be light"; and there was light. And God saw that the light was good; and God separated the light from the darkness. God called the light Day, and the darkness he called Night. And there was evening and there was morning, the first day.

 O God, help us to remember again the importance of words. With words you brought us into being. With words we give or take life from one another. We ask that you help us guard our words so that they will enable the best growth in our children. Amen.

Assignments for the Week

The most important work for this study will happen when you try what you've heard today in your own home.

1 Choose one of the Four Commandments to focus on. Look for ways this advice helps improve communication within the family this week.

2 Catch yourself in at least one "Conversation Stopper" and change your normal response.

Remember that you can call another parent in the group for support, ideas, or celebration.

Emotions

About this session:

Teenagers are a cauldron of seething emotions, bubbling and ready to boil over one minute and calm the next. This session will help you make sense of some of the mix, and help you teach them how to stir the pot carefully.

Goals to help you:

Consider the range of feelings with which teens and adults cope;
Identify your own feelings and the feelings of teens;
Talk to teens about feelings;
Develop ideas to help teens express feelings in an acceptable, healthy way.

Opening Prayer

Loving God who placed us in families, we call upon you for help and guidance as we live together each day. Diffuse and direct our anger. Shine your hope into our sadness. Help us carry our griefs. And rejoice with us when we are glad. Amen.

The five primary emotions are mad, glad, sad, scared, and hurt. Other feelings are a blend of two or more of these. Recognizing that your teen might be both glad and scared about a success or mad and sad and hurt about a loss can help talk through the mix of feelings.

Five Primary Feelings

 Mad

 Glad

 Sad

 Scared

 Hurt

1 **Create an environment where all feelings are important.**

2 **Accept the fact that your teen has stated his or her real feelings at a particular moment.**

3 **Help youth name their feelings.**

4 **Know your own feelings.**

Mirroring Emotions with Your Teen

Mirror: Restate the feelings to make sure you understand. "I can see that you are frustrated and disappointed."

Validate: Let your teen know that his or her feelings are important. "You've been working hard and hoped to be driving next month. It makes sense that this is hard to take."

Emphasize: Tell him you care. "I would be frustrated too. I couldn't wait to get my license."

Your Teen's Emotional Development: A Road Map

This chart of the typical teen's emotional development will help you understand the many natural changes in your teen and his or her emotional capabilities as the teen approaches adulthood.*

10-year-old. The golden year between childhood and adolescence—
Feels especially good about self and the world;
Enjoys and takes pride in family.

11-year-old. Experiences stress and anxiety about growing up;
Begins to separate from parental influences and challenge parent's views;
More confused and argumentative; hard to live with at times;
May feel picked on;
Builds strong friendships with other children;
Is increasingly capable as a person.

12-year-old. Is more friendly and at ease;
More confident about growing up.

13-year-old. More contemplative, searching for own identity;
Becomes more sensitive to teasing and criticism;
Needs more privacy.

14-year-old. Generally more at ease with demands of adolescence;
Seems more personally content;
Has better, more satisfying personal relationships.

15-year-old. Feels anxious about soon joining adult world and leaving home, but anticipates more freedom;
Wants, needs to make his or her own decisions;
May become less open and talkative at home;
Spends more time with friends.

16-year-old. More at ease with self;
Acts more responsibly, feels satisfied with gains in independence;

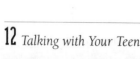

Feels on fairly equal footing with adults.
*Information presented on this chart applies to boys and girls alike.

Helps for Handling Teen Emotions at Home

▲ Be there.
▲ Take opportunites when they come.
▲ Create a family center in your home.
▲ Allow bad news.
▲ Prepare and share meals.
▲ Encourage relationships with other responsible adults at church or school.

Shoulder-to-Shoulder Tasks vs. Face-to-Face Conversations

Looking into your teen's eyes when you talk about important topics is priceless. There is also a place for "shoulder-to-shoulder" time. Sharing a task together, side-by-side, like preparing a meal, working on the car, or running, is very important for teens. This low-pressure time, particularly for teen boys, can make talking easier.

Stoppers or Common Mistakes to Avoid

The following are common mistakes parents are susceptible to, particularly in times of high emotion and anxiety. It's common when dealing with intense emotions to either become anxious or try to quickly make the tension go away. Here are six common reactions to begin to avoid.

▲ **Don't get drawn in.** Parents should not allow themselves to mirror their teen's anger. You stand a much better chance of defusing the situation if you make a conscious choice not to become angry as well.

▲ **Don't give in.** Withstand the teen's intense anger while holding him to the responsible course—it's your job. That does not mean never to reconsider a position or admit you have been wrong. It means that when you insist that a teen behave responsibly and impose consequences if he doesn't, anger may follow.

▲ **Don't fold your arms.** Open your arms, both figuratively and literally. Folded arms indicate a cold, judging, closed stance, while open arms are welcoming, loving, and protective.

▲ **Don't ignore other factors.** Look for a pattern. What else is going on here? Is your teen exhausted? Is she hungry? Does he know how to do what you have asked him to do?

▲ **Don't mistake your own defensiveness for your teen's.** It is important to figure out why some things about your teen bug you. Examine the issues that make you defensive. Learn to recognize your "hot buttons."

Dealing with Anger/Frustration

When parents of teens talk about emotions (and they often do), anger seems to be the most frequently mentioned and the hardest to handle. Let your teens know: "It is OK to be and feel angry, but you are responsible for your acts. It isn't OK to abuse yourself, someone else, or property." The following will help your teen express anger in appropriate ways:

1 Set boundaries around what can be said in anger. Teens will want to complain, whine, and shout at times. Allow the complaining with some rules. One rule that may work for you is saying, "You can yell about the rules. You can really hate what I'm telling you, but it is not appropriate for you to say you hate me."

2 Make available other appropriate ways to vent anger and the energy that comes with it. Try the following:
▲ Punching a punching bag;
▲ Writing about the situation;
▲ Playing a musical keyboard or other instrument;
▲ Engaging in physical exercise;
▲ Tackling a chore like mowing the yard.

Trouble Signs

When do anger or other strong emotions signal trouble? Watch for these warning signs:
▲ Withdrawing from friends;
▲ Plunging grades;
▲ Disturbing behaviors;
▲ Obsessive-compulsive behaviors;
▲ Self-destructive behavior (binging, purging, cutting, piercing);
▲ Obsession with fire;
▲ Abusing animals or other living things.

The National Mental Health Association estimates that one in eight teens suffer from depression. Further, depression can contribute to eating disorders, a type of illness that frequently affects teenage girls. The eating disorder may also be the underlying cause of the depression. The symptoms of semi-starvation and depression are remarkably similar—lack of interest, poor concentration, sleep disturbances, and lethargy.

Romans 12: 14-18

Bless those who persecute you; bless and do not curse them. Rejoice with those who rejoice, weep with those who weep. Live in harmony with one another; do not be haughty, but associate with the lowly; do not claim to be wiser than you are. Do not repay anyone evil for evil, but take thought for what is noble in the sight of all. If it is possible, so far as it depends on you, live peaceably with all.

 God of all life, be with us in our anger, our fears, our anxieties. Help us manage our emotions appropriately. Help us to raise emotionally healthy teens. Now help us feel your presence and your guidance as we go to our homes to live with what we have learned this week. Amen.

Assignment for the Week

1 Look this week for ways to create more space for time together in your home. Try at least one family meal together. During the meal, discuss together feelings you've had during that day, using the mirroring technique.

2 This week find a task you can do with your teen. This could be preparing a meal, doing family chores, or running errands in the car. During the task, talk together about ways to handle anger. Share one technique you use and ask your teen one technique they currently use or would like to try.

Chapter Three

Respect

About this session:

Respect (or lack of it) lies at the core of all human interaction. Parents want and expect respect. This session will help parents respect themselves and their teen as persons of worth, and begin to build the respect they deserve in the family.

Goals to help you:
Develop a definition of respect that parents verbalize and share with their teens;
Outline practical steps for building more respectful family relationships;
Learn to deal positively with disrespectful behavior.

Opening Prayer

Loving God, the one who so merits respect, we are reminded how through Jesus you continue to show love and respect for your creation. Help us to so reflect your love that through our actions our children see themselves as respected individuals. Keep us ever mindful of what we model, knowing that our actions are the ones our children use to judge what is respectful behavior. Now guide us in this time of learning and growing together. Amen.

The Positive Side of Respect in the Ten Commandments

The Ten Commandments are a basic guide for respectful living. Like many rules, most of the commandments are expressed in terms of negative behavior to avoid. Whether scriptural or household, rules and boundaries have a negative to avoid and an implicit positive to encourage. What is the positive activity within the "No" of the commandments?

About Respect for God
You shall have no other gods before me.
You shall not make for yourself a graven image.
You shall not take the name of the Lord your God in vain.
Remember the Sabbath day and keep it holy.

About Family/ Authority
Honor your father and your mother.

Human Interaction
You shall not kill.
You shall not commit adultery.
You shall not steal.
You shall not bear false witness against your neighbor.
You shall not covet your neighbor's house.

Helps for Building Respect

We've talked about the definition of respect. What about what respect *isn't?*

Here are some statements to remember:

▲ Respect is not idealization: we want our kids to respect us, yet with the knowledge of our inadequacies.

▲ Respect is not popularity. While we can be friends with our children, we still have to remember the boundaries and know we are there for a different role. BE A PARENT!

Respect is about being a leader and setting an example for your children. How do you begin to build a respectful relationship with your children?

1 Kids watch the way we interact with others. Sometimes what we do or say communicates a lack of respect for a group of people or a particular person.

2 How do we interact with our spouse or ex-spouse?

3 Teens learn from the story of a parent's life. Talk to your teen about your life, your experiences, and your choices, both good and bad.

4 The Golden Rule (Matthew 7:12) is the simplest statement of mutual respect in the world: treat everybody the way you want to be treated.

5 Respect yourself, your own needs and your own abilities.

6 Be consistent and unified.

7 Teaching your teen about respect is unavoidable! Live out the respect you expect from your teen.

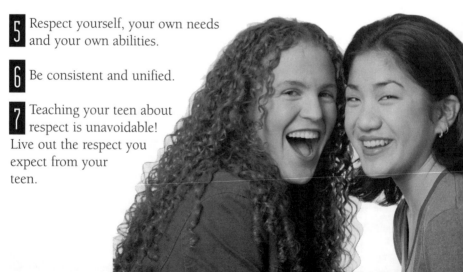

Remember, one day, sooner or later, your teenager will try to convince you that you are a lousy parent. He or she may even draw you into a situation where you will be persuaded that she or he is right. But you are still the parent, still the authority figure in the family. Try to be loving, even though you might not feel much love in return at that particular time. Check your response with another adult. Call a friend or talk with your spouse about the situation. Ask for adult support when support from your child may not be forthcoming.

Dealing with Disrespect

How we deal with disrespectful behavior after it has happened is just as important as setting up rules to prevent its happening.

So, what happens when the rule is broken and a teen has been disrespectful? Parents have to learn not to respond emotionally to disrespect. It is natural to respond emotionally, so keeping that under control is an unnatural act. We have to train ourselves not to respond, but to reflect.
▲ Try the familiar count-to-ten response.
▲ Don't take personally what has been said. Don't lash out, if you don't want your teen to react that way to you. Calmly state, "You do not have the right to speak to me that way. That makes me feel bad. I would not say that to you." In that way, you restate the family principle of mutual respect.
▲ If your teen does not respond positively at that point, you may have to impose consequences.
▲ What does it all mean? Beyond the anger or frustration, try to figure out what your child is trying to tell you.

Philippians 1:3-5
I thank my God every time I remember you, constantly praying with joy in every one of my prayers for all of you, because of your sharing in the gospel from the first day until now.

Closing Prayer **Loving God, we are awed by your love and joy in us. We humbly receive this love and ask that you guide each of us in being a beacon of love in our families. Help us live lives of respect and gratitude for all that has been given to us. Amen.**

Assignment for the Week

1 Call a family meeting for this week. Review together as a family the spoken and unspoken rules for the family. Together write the rules for the family in positive terms, using respect for one another.

2 At home, have one parent agree to be the observer-listener. Check the other's parenting skills for one day. Then switch roles and have the other parent be the observer. If you are a single parent, ask your best friend to critique your interchanges with your teen.

How well do you listen when you're talking with your teen? When others are around, do you answer questions for your teen? Do you interrupt? Do you make positive or negative assumptions?

Success and Failure

Chapter Four

About this session:

Success and disappointments are intense experiences for teens. This session will help you consider your definitions of success. In this session, you will identify ways we measure success in ourselves, our teenagers, and our family. You will learn ways to encourage your teen to be and do their best.

Goals to help you:
Examine notions of success and failure;
Consider family priorities;
Set family goals around success;
Obtain specific ideas for dealing with success and failure.

Opening Prayer

Gracious God, when we reflect your goodness, cheer us on. When we fail and fall short, pick us up. Through all our days, help us to remain faithful to your purposes and your people, especially to the children you have placed in our care. Amen.

Teen Issues

1 **Teens can be harsh and even cruel to one another.** Your teen lives in that culture and may be made to feel like a failure more often than you realize. If teens perceive that no one at home cares, they will wonder what they did (or didn't do) that made no one care about or value them.

2 **Teens today are often exhausted.** Recent research on the teen brain tells us many teens need much more rest than they are getting. Teens need 9-10 hours of sleep a night. In our society, it is harder than ever for young persons to feel positive about themselves and incidents of real clinical depression and suicide have increased.

3 **Change is constant.** Teenagers experience major change almost daily. Consider the rapid changes in their height, weight, appearance, and voice. Think about the growth in mental and physical abilities. Consider the increased demands in the social and academic expectations over that which teens experienced 20 years ago. Think of how long it takes you, as an adult, to feel confident in a new role or job. Teens have not had much time to overcome doubt in the midst of rapid change and growth.

4 **Development differs.** People peak at different times. Teens seek to fit in and be like other teens. Because development differs, few see themselves as fitting in. Simply the way they are developing may contribute to their sense of personal success or failure. Your teen's strengths may not be valued now, at this stage in life, or may be late in developing.

When Failure Comes

We all make mistakes—it's part of being human. The question is how we learn from the experience and move on. Sometimes our failures can be our best growing experiences. Let's look at a list of practical ways we can help our children accept, learn from, and deal with failures.

1 Talk with your teen. Debrief the incident. Seek together to name the learnings from this incident. Make a list of those learnings. Actually write down the learnings. Figure out together how to use the new information to improve the outcome next time. This process will help the teen feel he or she has the power to improve, instead of feeling helpless and wanting to give up.

2 Brainstorm what your teen was seeking from this experience. List ways to receive this same success in other areas. For instance, if your teen has tried to make a new friend and been rejected, what would be other ways to approach making new friends? Help your teen examine his or her natural gifts and identify where their strengths lie.

3 Plan for success. Think ahead about what is needed to succeed. For example, whether the teen is trying to ace the math test or grab the rebounds in the big game tomorrow, he or she needs a good night's sleep. Would a couple of practice runs of tomorrow's speech, in front of the family, help with stage fright? Do everything you can in advance to increase the possibilities of success.

4 **Use humor.** Don't make fun or ridicule, but you can lighten the gravity of the situation. Do this with your own less-than-stellar performances, and your kids will see that it is possible to laugh off defeats. If you can laugh at yourself, your own failures, you send a powerful message that it's not the end of the world.

5 **Praise your child to others.** Hearing you praising one of your teen's good qualities or an important achievement to other family members or friends builds up the self-image of your teen.

Stepping in as a Parent—When Is It Necessary?

Most parenting authors agree that it is important to allow children to compete—to make the effort and experience successes and failures. Sometimes it is painful, as a parent, to experience these with your son or daughter.

When should you step in? Experiencing competition is good for teens—humiliation is not. Anticipate when a disaster seems to be looming. If you see your teen being set up to fail by a teacher or coach or choral director who has not allowed him or her time to be sufficiently prepared with the right information, speak up. Sometimes by doing your own homework as a parent, you can prevent traumatic consequences for your child.

Ask questions.
Check on the experience and training of the other participants.
Make sure you and your child understand the rules and expectations.
Be involved enough to know what is going on.
If it sounds, smells, or feels like a bad situation, step in.

Making it as a Parent

▲ **Make Time.** In their rushed existence, teens need to have important downtime, particularly with their family in the safety and reassurance of the home. As the family's management, it's up to parents to create that time in the schedule.

▲ **Put your children in touch with their family heritage.** Share the family legends, stories, and photographs.

Teens need to know how and to whom they belong. Do they have Uncle Jack's wit? Grandmother Allene's intuition? They also share in the membership of the family just by knowing these same stories. This storytelling helps to answer the fundamental question: Who are we as a family? Are we something special? unique? This helps shape the vision of the family as a "we."

▲ **Help insure that church is a welcoming place for teens.** If a teen comes to church and feels the same rejection he or she feels everywhere else, they will leave. Watch especially for elitism and cliques. These often form naturally but can be addressed by youth workers and parents. Parents are critical helps to the youth minister or leader in making church a haven.

▲ **Reward effort.** Give the congratulatory bouquet or decorated cake to celebrate the courage of the tryout, not after she or he gets the part. Award assists and rebounds as well as points. Remember to congratulate yourself on your parenting skills as well as your kids on all their endeavors.

▲ **Be present.** As often as you can, be present when your teen is competing, performing, or participating in important events. Be kind but honest about results. It is okay to acknowledge that perhaps this was not a teen's finest hour, especially if she or he already knows it. Empty praise when teens know they were off their form does not mean much.

▲ **Describe what you see.** Be descriptive, specific, and tell your feelings. Affirm the gifts and strengths you see.

Assignment for the Week

1 Find a time to share your memory of a success or failure you experienced as a teen with your teenager. Tell your teenagers you love them every day.

2 Together with your teen, watch one show on television. As you watch, look at what definitions of success and failure are being used in the show and in the commercials. Talk with your teen about how you wish to define success and failure in your family.

Chapter Five
Grief and Loss

About this session:

Teenagers experience losses of all kinds, from the breakup of a romance to the death of a parent. Grief is a journey that is experienced differently by each person. This session will provide parents with coping skills for the grief process and a theology of hope.

Goals to help you:
Recognize and acknowledge the different causes of grief;
Understand better how teens may deal with grief;
Receive practical helps for helping teens with death, divorce, and other losses.

Opening Prayer

Tender God who leads us through the valley of loss and shadows, give us your presence this day. Come near, that we may live in hope. Amen.

> "With my mother's death all settled happiness, all that was tranquil and reliable, disappeared from my life....It was sea and islands now; the great continent had sunk like Atlantis." (C. S. Lewis, on the death of his mother when he was 10 years old, *Surprised by Joy* [San Diego: Harcourt Brace Jovanovich, 1956]

Stages of Grief

For adults and teens, keep in mind the stages of the grief process. Though the five occur in sequence, they do not happen in tidy stages, one ending before the next one begins. Instead, the griever may wander back and forth among them randomly, with more or less intensity, with varying degrees of frequency, over a period of time.

Denial—"It hasn't happened; I won't think about it; everything can be the same."

Bargaining—"If only" or "What if." Teens may try to negotiate or trade to postpone or fix the problem.

Anger—"Why me?" Rage and hostility may be be directed at the family, God, the person who died or left, or at themselves. It's an important stage and can be healthy if the teen can find a healthy way to express his or her anger.

Resignation—"What's the use?" As the reality of the loss sets in, teens may experience both highs and lows coming to terms with it. They may feel depression and powerlessness.

Acceptance—"It may be OK." The teen begins to adapt to go on in the new situation. He or she begins to learn to live with the change.

Every person—child, adult, or teenager—grieves differently. We have different ways of expressing our emotion; and each circumstance brings its own unique issues. There are some traits in handling loss to keep in mind with all members of the family.

▲ **Teens feel immortal.** The child's age has a great impact on perception of death. In families, members of all ages will feel a loss or grief. Infants and toddlers will feel absence and sadness; children three to five years of age ask curious questions and may feel that death is reversible—that grandmother may come back; school age children are more likely to see death as concrete and permanent. Teens understand the science but feel death is something that always happens to other people. An unexpected death can shake a teen's illusions about the universe.

▲ **Everyone has a different timetable for handling a loss.** Even two siblings may need greatly varying times to recover from the same crisis. For major crises, keep in mind the calendar. Even if your child is handling loss well, remember that holidays, anniversaries, graduations—all the milestones of life will bring back the loss. Make a note of times to pay special attention.

▲ **Kids experience not only the loss but family change.** When grief affects the whole family, kids can get lost in the instability grief causes. They feel the uncertainty and are aware that the parent's energy is turned inward toward his or her own grief. In addition to grieving the original loss, then, the teenager must also grieve the loss of the parent's attention.

▲ **Teens may take breaks.** Something in a teen knows it's an enormous task just to grow up. In the face of such pressure, they grieve sporadically then go right back to growing up. They will dip in and out of the grieving process. For this reason, grief may be postponed and will certainly be extended.

▲ **If grief isn't expressed, it can manifest itself physically.**
A teen may not talk about sadness or express loss, but could have severe stomachaches, headaches, or trouble sleeping and eating. The body may be expressing the grief if the brain is not.

▲ **There are many ups and downs.** Grief is not like flu, where you get better day by day.

It's like waves, regressing then getting better, and regressing again. The wave cycle is the body's way of coping—the grief is too much to take in all at once. A person thinks, "I'm better," then WHAM! In families, sometimes family members will not be experiencing the ups and downs at the same times. That may be awkward unless the family understands the changes that are happening.

Helping a Teen Through Loss

There are some very practical things you can do to help ease the grief process. Here are some ideas.

1 Don't try to fix the emotions the way you would a scraped knee.

2 If the grief is something you share together, let your child see you grieve.

3 Help the teen feel in control. Maintain routine as much as possible. Don't abandon discipline just because everyone is sad.

4 Don't be afraid to laugh.

5 Touch and hold your teen every day.

6 If the loss is a major issue like death or divorce, be sure school personnel know what has happened so they can be supportive.

7 Seek out older people, like grandparents or family friends, for your child to spend time with. Their length of vision and perspective can help you and your teen.

8 Ask for help. Turn to friends who can help you with the fathering or mothering: shopping, house repair, chauffeuring—all the stuff of parenting and running a household.

9 Sometimes you don't even know what you need. The community can help. Just to know the church is still there worshiping provides stability and is a continuing source of comfort.

10 Do the best you can, day by day. Grief is not isolated from life; it is part of living. The well of sadness and well of joy are the same well.

Special Helps for Dealing with Death

The loss of a loved grandparent, a peer, or particularly a parent or sibling is a defining experience for a young person. Here are a few helps to consider when talking with your child about death.

▲ Don't try to protect teens with vague language. Avoid euphemisms. Use specific words like *death*.
▲ Be specific: answer what is being asked. Tell the truth—no half-truths, no fairy tales. It's okay to say "I don't know" or "I'm not comfortable answering that now; let me think about what I want to say."
▲ Share what you believe—talk to your pastor to help clarify your own beliefs about a Christian's view of death and afterlife.
▲ Don't express death as "the will of God" or blame God. Saying that God needed a loved one in heaven could cause resentment toward God in a grieving teen.
▲ Help your teen look for other young people who have experienced death. One teen told people her parents were divorced because she didn't know anyone else whose father had died.

To Honor the Deceased

▲ Talk about the loved one. Tell the stories. Listen to your teen's stories about the deceased. Bear in mind that the stories are told not to inform, but to believe. When people believe the story, they can quit telling it.
▲ Look at scrapbooks. Keep pictures around. Allow the teen to have an article of clothing—a symbol of the loved one.
▲ Use physical symbols. Plant a tree or flowers. Display the flag that draped the coffin of a veteran. Wear, or on occasion allow your teen to wear, a piece of jewelry that belonged to the loved one. Objects can lead to ways to talk about the person.

The Grief of Divorce

Divorce always brings a grieving process, even in cases where everyone acknowledges that the divorce is a necessary step. There is still the death of a dream and the loss of structure for the child. Kids are always powerless in divorce. They have no decision-making power in a situation where their lives are going to be radically altered. Regardless of how well or badly the adults behave themselves, the children of divorce have grieving to do.

Children and teens need to mourn the unified family life they have lost. Teens may react with anger, but often that anger is fear in disguise.

Here are some suggestions for parents in helping teens deal with divorce:

▲ Provide ongoing structure—establish a workable daily routine so that your teens know where they are supposed to be and what they are to be doing. Don't forget to build some "free time" into the schedule, and to allow for some flexibility.

▲ Keep your word. If you say you will be at your child's ball game, be there. If you say you will be coming home at 6:00 P.M., be on time.

▲ Always let your child know where you are and how you can be reached by telephone, beeper, or cell phone.

▲ Encourage contact with the other parent. Give a teenager stamps, stationery, and a personal address book including the other parent's mailing and e-mail address and phone number.

▲ Tell the child in what (positive) ways she or he reminds you of the other parent.

Romans 8:38-39.

For I am convinced that neither death, nor life, nor angels, nor rulers, nor things present, nor things to come, nor powers, nor height, nor depth, nor anything else in all creation, will be able to separate us from the love of God in Christ Jesus our Lord.

Closing Prayer

God who guides us day by day, help us know and experience your love and care in the worst of times and in the best of times. Help us be aware of those times when our children grieve. Help us be parents who can respond to our child's grief and loss. Surround us with your love and care in those hurting times. Remind us in loving ways of the needs our teens have to hear how we love and care for them every day, but also particularly during their times of grief and loss. Amen.

Assignment for the Week

1 Interview your own parents or other family relatives about their grief and sad times. Take time this week to sit down with your youth and tell them the family stories you remember.

2 Interview your teen this week. Ask:
▲ What do teens wish parents knew about loss and grief?
▲ Do you have any friends who are going through rough times now?
▲ Do you have a friend who needs special pareyer or attention now.

Remember, every day, touch your kid with affection and say "I love you."

Sexuality

Chapter Six

About this session:

Parents worry about it. Kids think about it and wonder and fantasize about it. It pervades sitcoms and advertising and music. It is a simple fact of life, perhaps even *the* fact of life. This session will help parents be more at ease with their teen's sexuality: the changes in their bodies, the development of romantic feelings, emerging interpersonal relationships, and the added responsibilities of maturity.

Goals to help you:

Understand the importance of an open communication channel;
Be able to talk comfortably with your teen about sex and sexuality;
Know what to expect at different stages of development;
Know how to help your teen live in an R-rated world.

Not My Kid!

Kids become very aware and often preoccupied with sexuality at twelve or thirteen. It's all new. All children need help from parents in dealing with this new and powerful influence.

▲ **Do not assume that this lesson does not apply to you.** Teens are having sex younger and with more and more partners. The average age of first intercourse in the United States is 16, and 66% of high school seniors have intercourse before they graduate (Centers for Disease Control and Prevention, *Morbidity and Mortality World Report,* 45[55], [(September 1996)] 16-19).

▲ **Know that sound, basic information, available from you at different times and in different settings, is always good.** Don't worry that providing facts will encourage your teen's sexual exploration. Knowing more, particularly about emotional and health affects, may well lead a teen to wait.

In school-based programs, research shows that prevention programs that include information about delaying intercourse and about contraception can delay the beginning of sexual activity, reduce the frequency of intercourse, and decrease the number of teens' sexual partners (A. Grunseit and S. Krippax, *Effects of Sex Education on Young People's Sexual Behaviour.* [World Health Organization, 1994]).

Starting the Conversation

Few parents are experts on sex education, but you can find resources written by experts and share them with your teen. As a parent, however, the best thing you can do for your teen is to be available, open, and willing to talk.

▲ **Talk with your teens about sex and sexuality.** Talk on more than one occasion. If you don't feel equipped to answer all their questions, find a good book, read it, and make it available to them. They have the right to good information—and they also need to know that sex is not a taboo or awkward topic with their parent.

▲ **Provide the facts.** By age nine or ten, kids know a little and have heard a lot, much of it misinformation. If you don't provide help, your teen's portfolio may be a mix of facts and fiction from friends, dates, movies, or magazines.

▲ **Set a matter-of-fact tone.** Teens want to talk through these matters – hopefully with you. They want and deserve honest, realistic answers. Openness with teens will be easier if they feel they can ask you anything without shock, jumping to conclusions, or fear.

▲ **Abstinence is not the only focus.** You hope that by providing information and support, your child will decide to wait until maturity and marriage. Make sure it is the reasons behind abstinence that are the value. To promote that sex before marriage is just wrong won't have much power with many teens. Telling them the reasons for waiting—time to grow and mature, the pain of breaking up an intimate relationship, and learning to love and care for yourself first, valuing yourself—are powerful. It's true that God created sexuality for the bonds of a committed permanent relationship—talk with them about why.

▲ **Don't assume that your teen will be the one to wait.** In the end, it will always be his or her own decision. Help your teens by giving them the information they need to make decisions grounded in faith, facts, emotional understanding, and maturity.

▲ **Tell them it's more than facts.** Talk to teens about the deep intimacy and emotions of sex. A sexual relationship creates energy that the teen may not be equipped to handle. Instill an understanding of the power of sexuality.

▲ **Finally, allow some freedom.** As your teen approaches high school graduation, begin to give him or her a little more freedom. If your son or daughter can begin to experience making choices in the safe and supportive home environment, when he goes away to college, he is less apt to go to extremes with new-found freedom.

The overriding goal here is to provide good support for your child. If this seems particularly tough, find good books and resources, ask a trusted aunt, uncle, or other relative to step in or start a sexuality education program at the church led by a trained practitioner. If you need more help, it might be a good investment to visit with a family therapist who can help you think through the conversation and provide one-on-one support.

Keeping Cool with Hot Topics

Unless you are a professional counselor, talking through your teen's questions about sex will have tense moments. Here are some tips that may help:

▲ **Don't overreact.** When surprising questions on sexuality arise, don't jump to conclusions. Do your best to answer the questions honestly. Ask if there was a reason for the question.

▲ **Don't be afraid to admit embarrassment.** Allow for some laughter, blushing, and squirming. Acknowledging your own embarrassment will help diffuse your teen's discomfort. Let him know that, although you may both be uncomfortable, this is important enough to do.

▲ **Don't default on supervision.** Your teen will need guidance and parenting as well as information. Be upfront with your teens if you're concerned about the time they spend alone with their boyfriend or girlfriend. A lot of time, alone and unsupervised, with someone they really like will make it tough for them to make good decisions.

Keep in mind after-school time as well as nighttime curfews. Counselors tell us that experimentation with drinking, drugs, and sex often begins between three and six o'clock, free time between school and parents' return home. Have rules about who can be in the house when you are not home and enforce them.

▲ **Don't scare your teen into waiting.** Tell the facts about health, STDs, AIDS, and pregnancy; but also share the beauty and joy of a loving relationship.

▲ **Don't pretend that physical expression isn't important.** Teens can enjoy a physical interaction without sexual intimacy. Hugging, kissing, and playful horseplay can fulfill some of the need for touch. Encourage group activities. Encourage actively doing things together with their dates and friends; **don't let their increasing physical intimacy exploration become the focus of their time together.**

▲ Don't pretend a decision hasn't been made.

Surprising as it may sound, teens need to admit it when they have made a decision to become sexually active. Some kids don't want to use contraceptives because that means admitting they planned to have sex. It eliminates the "I couldn't help myself; it won't happen again" defense.

This is tough as a parent—especially when you see how hurtful their choice can be for their lives. You can take a stand and say: Intercourse is best when you're older and in marriage, but if you make a different choice, then we expect responsibility – responsibility for your health and that of your partner and responsible reliable birth control.

Ages and Stages of Sexual Interest

Parents often voice concern about what constitutes "normal" curiosity. The generalized stages listed below are normal stages for teens to pass through, and they outline patterns of normal curiosity and behavior.

Approximate Age Group Common Behaviors

10 years: Considerable interest in "smutty" jokes. Interested in reading books about sex and babies. Girls begin to experience some body changes.

11 years: Girls are interested in knowing more about intercourse, but reticent in talking about it with mother. Boys' information is gathered from other boys.

12 years: Most rapid growth in both height and weight. Menstrual periods begin. Both sexes want information.

13 years: Primarily concerned with own development. Am I keeping pace with my friends? By this time, boys may be experiencing their first ejaculation whether through dreams or masturbation.

14 years: Intensely concerned with body build. Interested in aspects of reproduction—contraceptives, miscarriage. Further sex education is needed and eagerly received, including information on physiology and functioning of sex parts, intercourse, birth control, unwanted pregnancy, sexually transmitted diseases, herpes, AIDS, prostitution, abortion, and homosexuality.

Prepare teens for the upcoming changes in their bodies before they begin to happen. Keep in mind the differences between development in boys and in girls. The first major changes for girls, developing breasts and hips, are very visible. For boys, the noticeable changes, like facial hair and height, happen later. The first changes for boys, in penis size and first ejaculation, aren't as obvious.

Especially For Daughters

What are the emotional risks of early sexual experience? Author Mary Pipher, in *Reviving Ophelia*, sees tangible harm to young women. "I see the unhappiness of early sexual intimacy—the sadness and anger at rejection, the pain over bad reputations, the pregnancies, the health problems and the cynicism of girls who have had every conceivable sexual experience except a good one. ... most early sexual activity in our culture tends to be harmful to girls." (*Reviving Ophelia: Saving the Souls of Adolescent Girls*, [New York: Ballantine, 1994], 208).

▲ Listen to Mary Pipher's condensation of Ophelia's life from *Hamlet*.

"As a girl, Ophelia is happy and free, but with adolescence she loses herself. When she falls in love with Hamlet, she lives only for his approval. She has no inner direction; rather she struggles to meet the demands of Hamlet and her father. Her value is determined utterly by their approval. Ophelia is torn apart by her efforts to please." (*Reviving Ophelia*, p. 20)

▲ Does that sound familiar to any of you?
▲ As a mother, are you affirming any of these ideas?
▲ Can you identify with that?
▲ As a father, can you identify with any of this?
▲ Can your daughters?

Ways to Help

▲ Boys can be horribly cruel, particularly during the middle-school years. Other girls, though rarely ridiculing boys, can be equally cruel to each other. Talk to your teen about respect and empathy for others.

▲ Parents of boys need to teach their sons respect and empathy for the girls in their age group.

▲ Mothers of girls can be role-models for their daughters, exampling self-respect, self-reliance, and good values.

▲ Parents, particularly fathers, can be a strong foundation for their daughters during these changes. Some fathers may feel less comfortable in hugging and horseplay when they see their child turning into a young woman. Daughters need approval, support, and affection from their fathers in this time of uncertainty about their appearance and identity. Strong relationships at home may help reduce the need for constant approval outside the home.

▲ Cultural treatment of women is a true danger to our teens. Eating disorders and body-image problems are rampant in girls as young as ten years old. The pressure to reflect the ideal can leave girls believing:

> Sexuality is dependent on being attractive;
> My body is good only if it fits the world's definition of attractive;
> My body is attractive only if it is skinny.

The most popular girls in middle school are often the skinniest. Our culture presents models and movie stars who are willowy at best, and at worst, anorexic. The Barbie-doll standard is creating a preoccupation that is unprecedented.

Especially For Sons

Young men have their own social and cultural pressures. In teen years, boys may be constantly comparing themselves to their peers—are they growing as fast, are they developing as quickly, who's shaving?

▲ Talk to your son as he grows up about your definition of masculinity. What does it mean to "be a man"? What images is he seeing and hearing from the world around him? Where does he place caring, responsibility, accountability, and grace?

▲ Listen for the pressure he feels from peers to move faster. Boys are pushed by other boys to claim more sexual adventure and experience. They may even feel pressure from the girls they date. Don't think that only your daughters are being pressured to rush intimacy.

▲ Fathers can model respect, vulnerability, and a willingness for intimacy especially in relationships with their spouse. Let your son see affection between you and your wife. Many of us don't like to disagree in front of our children, but sometimes allow your teen to see you and your spouse work through a disagreement. As long as the disagreement doesn't escalate, seeing you respectfully work through a misunderstanding is good modeling behavior.

▲ Boys may not be as prepared to talk about and manage their emotions. Parents, particularly fathers or other male role models, can help sons name and talk about their feelings. Teen boys may readily express anger but have trouble understanding why they feel the frustration and have trouble working through it.

▲ Talking with boys, parents might try more "shoulder-to-shoulder" time. Many young men are more comfortable talking about tough issues while working with you on an activity rather than the more pressurized, face-to-face setting.

 Closing Prayer **Loving God, we are yours. Help us to use this gift of creation in ways pleasing to you. Help us to be open doors of communication with our youth. Keep us in your care as we leave this place this week. Remind us daily of your love and care. Amen.**

Assignment for the Week

Spend some time this week, with your spouse or a close friend, writing down the messages you would most want to convey to your teen about love, sex, and sexuality. Think about:

> What did I learn from my first real experience with love?
> What do I wish my own parents had told me?
> If I could list the three most important messages for my teen, what would they be?